Published by Anthology of Poetry, Inc.

©*Anthology of Poetry by Young Americans*®
1998 Edition
Volume LXXX
All Rights Reserved©

Printed in the United States of America

To submit poems
for consideration in the 1999 edition of the
Anthology of Poetry by Young Americans®,
send to:

> Anthology of Poetry, Inc.
> PO Box 698
> Asheboro, NC 27204-0698

Authors responsible
for originality of poems submitted.

The Anthology of Poetry, Inc.
307 East Salisbury • P.O. Box 698
Asheboro, NC   27204-0698

ISBN: 1-883931-13-4

Anthology of Poetry by Young Americans®
is a registered trademark of
Anthology of Poetry, Inc.

The poetry in the 1998 edition of the *Anthology of Poetry by Young Americans*® continues our nine year tradition of publishing a diverse and eclectic volume of children's poetry. Our poets come from all over the United States, from children in kindergarten to seniors in high school. They come from all the different social, economic, religious and philosophical backgrounds possible, but they all share with us a snapshot of some part of their lives or thoughts. The works of art represented here give us a picture of our children only possible with the vivid and colorful language of poetry We tried to present the poems as the author wrote them, in their format and punctuation.

In response to the numerous requests we received to dedicate this years anthology to the "Year of the Ocean", we have covered the volume in a deep blue. We would like to extend a special thanks to all the poets who participated. We are expecting great things from them in the future.

The Editors

THE CHRISTMAS CHEER

Christmas is my favorite time of year
With all the lights and holiday cheer
Santa Claus in his suit of red
"What would you like for Christmas?" he said.
Presents wrapped under the tree
Some for you and some for me.
Candy, stockings, and gifts are fun
This day is also for a special one.
Remember, Jesus was born on this day
That is why we celebrate every year this way.

James R. Brown

I LIKE CANDY

I like the name Mandy.
Because it rhymes with candy.
I love sweets.
Mom gives us lots of treats.
Pop, chips, and candy.
I love them all.
If you have any candy just give me a call.
Vegetables are dandy,
But I would rather have candy.
That's why I like the name Mandy.
Because it rhymes with candy.

Amanda N. Pinson
Age: 9

DAY'S END

It's night outside;
I see the moon.
This day was over
Much too soon.
The whole world's quiet --
Not a peep.
It's time for me
To go to sleep.

Laci McKinney
Age: 9

MOMS

Moms are sweet.
Moms are nice.
Moms are made of sugar and spice.
Sometimes they get mad but mostly glad.
They fix us dinner every night
and they always make sure we eat right.
I guess that's why my mom, your mom,
everyone's mom was put on this earth
to make sure that we were brought up right
and that we sleep tight every night.

Tara O'Neal

WILD FLOWERS

Dried or pressed, fresh ones are best,
In a book or decorating a vest.
Some are big while others small,
Then there are those that can grow very tall.

Studied or admired,
Looking at them never makes you tired.
Common or rare,
Most of these plants make people stare.

Colors of red, yellow, blue, and pink,
Some smell good while others stink.
They all grow from various seeds,
However, some are considered weeds.

These plants all sprout in different seasons,
For this I can think of no good reasons.
Thistles, goldenrod, Queen Anne's Lace,
They wave in the wind with gentle grace.

What are these plants I am talking about?
They will die very quickly in a long hot drought.
Of course, they are the wonderful wild flowers,
And just like me, they love spring rain showers.

Amber M. Fannin
Age: 11

THE EVERYTHING TREE

Once there was a very special tree,
It gave its gifts only to me.
I have known this to be true since I was born,
That is why its bark with hugs it is worn.

In the hot afternoon, it provides me with shade,
From the hands of God, not manmade.
When to its trunk I brought my friends,
Cooling shade only to us it would lend.

The tree allowed me to climb it all,
From the low branches, to the ones higher than a mall.
On its limbs I like to swing,
Sometimes in the fall, summer, or spring.

Autumn brings me big apples that are bright,
I love to eat them in the night.
Spring apple blossoms brought a buzzing bee,
Pollinating buds to give fresh fruit to me.

To cut down this tree would be a crime,
For it has been with me for such a long time.
So to my tree, you must always be kind,
Because it brings forth treasures which are hard to find.

John C. Calhoun
Age: 9

AUTUMN LEAVES

In autumn the leaves begin to fall,
Their colors are the most beautiful of all.
These colorful leaves are autumn's pride.
The hues of the forest are too lovely to hide.

The leaves in the fall misty mountains,
Are like a rich rainbow fountain.
I look around me up so high,
To see the leaves light up the sky.

These leaves are scattered all around,
Some are red, others orange, yellow, or even brown.
Raking the leaves is a favorite chore,
Because I love being part of the great outdoors.

Leaves drift and dance around my head,
Falling to the cold, dark earth instead.
Shapes are many as they drop to the ground,
Long, short, wide, thin, and even round.

Velvety smooth are these glorious leaves,
Which I consider the most beautiful part of the tree.
In the evening sky, when the sun sets,
The reflection of light is the most splendid yet.

Sara M. Welter
Age: 9

HALLOWEEN

Scary, scary Halloween,
Witches and their cats are always seen.
You're sure to see a vampire or two,
And you can always count on a ghost to say "Boo!"

Goblins are all around,
Leaving their dark and muddy ground.
Mummies and phantoms are in your sight,
But what do you expect on Halloween night?

For it is the time of the living dead,
Just be thankful you still have your head.
For Halloween night is a frightful time,
You could wind up green and covered with slime.

I can't explain how horrible it is,
But time passes fast just like a whiz.
I go house to house with my bag,
So people can fill it until it sags.

Frankenstein and his wife might be there,
And a werewolf that is covered with hair.
Don't let this be a fright,
Because this won't be your last Halloween night.

Daniel Zane Clevenger
Age: 9

LEAVES

Leaves are falling
To the ground.
Wherever you look
There's more to be found.

Orange, yellow, and red
Brighten up the sky.
They look just like
They've been tie-dyed.

The trees are bare.
The air gets cool.
The days get shorter
And it's back to school.

The nights come early.
The sun goes down.
When autumn leaves,
I'm sure I'll frown.

Kayla King
Age: 12

AUTUMN IS THE BEST

Autumn is crazy and autumn is fun.
Autumn is season number one.
The best way to have fun
when all the leaves fall,
is condense them in a pile
jump in, you'll have a ball!

Late in the day, fatigue will kick in.
And bedtime rolls around about a quarter to ten.
That night when you are asleep,
dream about football and
becoming famously unique.

The next morning descend to the table
where food is ready and eating is able.
Then go out and disguise a man
to scare away crows.
Autumn is the best season
now everyone knows.

When you're playing in the snow
and thinking of the leaves,
Remember them as falling off the trees.
And when you are crying and sobbing for them,
Remember they are your best friends.

Les Colegrove
Age: 12

FALL

It's fall! It's fall!
The leaves are dropping.
At football games the leaves
under my feet are popping.

The leaves are on the ground
But not too much in the trees.
Grass is turning brown
just like the leaves.

It gets really cold
And you know winter is near.
With snow coming with it
and all kinds of cold weather I fear.

But hey, it's not so bad!
When it snows, we get out
And at football games
we will win out.

Jason Salyers
Age: 11

FALL

It's the beginning of fall.
The leaves on the trees are still tall.
With each day that comes around.
More leaves fall to the ground.

The wind and air are strong and brisk.
Going sleeveless is a risk.
Red, yellow, orange and brown,
Things are changing all around.

It's the fall season.
Which is the reason
For all the cheers and school spirit.
Just listen, can't you hear it?

The wind is strong
the air is brisk.
Sometimes the days
Are just a mist.
Red, yellow, orange and brown.
Things are changing all around.

Ashley Dawn Easterling
Age: 11

FALL

Fall is coming very soon.
So Mom will look at the branches
and make my dad prune.
Fall is a pleasant time of year,
there's Thanksgiving, Halloween and
Uncle Tom hunts deer.

Everyone is cleaning up all over town.
They're raking up leaves that have turned brown.
It's getting chillier as the leaves
are falling.
And soon there will be snow that
is appalling.

And oh, yes, fall brings
Halloween.
Ghosts, goblins, and other scary things.
We have spiderwebs to decorate the houses,
and little kids dress up like
monster mouses.

I enjoy October the most.
There's holiday parties and I get
to be the host.
Fall is the best season around,
to have fun with the colorful leaves
that fall on the ground.

Vanessa VanHoose
Age: 11

LEAVES

I never thought about the leaves,
That grow upon the branches of the trees.
Until my teacher helped me see
Just how very important they are to me.

I gathered leaves from many trees,
I wondered what they were.
I got some books looked them up
Hoping I could please her.

Some were easy, others were hard,
Some were fun to find.
I searched around looked up and down,
'Til it almost blew my mind.

The leaves were green and others were brown,
In trees and on the ground,
If you listen in the wind,
The leaves will make a sound.

My work is over, the project is done,
The leaves are all labeled and put in wax.
I've learned about leaves while having some fun,
While my fingers have been worked to the max.

Thomas Nicholas Tolliver
Age: 9

12

LEAVES, BEAUTIFUL LEAVES

Mother Nature, thank you for our trees,
Without them it would be impossible to breathe.
These tall plants wave their leaves at me,
Without saying good-bye, they give me a great breeze.

In the pretty old spring.
The leaves of trees grow light green.
Climbing up the branches high,
A nest I spy close to the sky.

Summer is a busy time for me,
Because I play tag around the tree.
The leaves of this plant are much darker,
Looking like a new green marker.

In the autumn the leaves do fall,
My poor tree has lost them all.
He is standing straight and bare,
There are no leaves upon him anywhere.

In the cold winter my tree does sleep.
Even the birds do not make a peep.
Under the branches a bunny of snow I make,
To keep my tree safe until it wakes.

Joshua T. Smith
Age: 9

FALL TIMES

I like fall,
Most colorful time of all.
The leaves dry up
And they start to fall.

When they dry up,
I like to rake them
all up.
Then I play
and lie in them.
When they are down to the ground.

I love the leaves.
I love the colors.
I love to play in the leaves
With my mother and father.

When I'm done,
I bag them all up.
I'll put on my jacket
And load them into the truck.

Allison E. Evans
Age: 12

WHAT WILL YOU BE?

On Halloween what will you be?
A witch, a ghost, or a pirate at sea.
Will you trick-or-treat
On your local street?

Will you go to town,
And see a big clown;
Or maybe see a witch,
Who has a big switch.

You might see a ghost
It's the character I like most.
You might see a princess, nice and sweet,
And she might give you a tasty treat.

These are some things you might see,
If you celebrate Halloween with me.
So have a good time and don't forget,
The more you give the more you can expect.

Megan Blanton
Age: 9

My name is George
and here is my life
great and sly
sharp as a knife.

I have but one hobby,
reading Greek Mythology.

My favorite sport
is not on the court,
it is with a brown ball
called football.

I have black hair
tall as a bear,
I have brown eyes
that will never die.

The colors that I like
are purple, black, and green
they're the colors of my bike.

And last my favorite treat
is something good to eat
pizza that is pepperoni
and my drink that is Pepsi.

George Lee Scott Jr
Age: 11

DOLPHINS

Dolphins live in the deep.
They leap in a glee.
They eat fish and shrimp.
When they eat too much they look like a blimp.
They jump out of the water,
Do neat tricks,
That's what dolphins do.

Brandon Scott Phipps
Age: 12

CHARACTERISTICS

My name is Brandon
I have brown hair, blue eyes
I am 5 foot 1 inch

I like Nike shoes
Black and white
They fit just right
When I'm running they will not hurt my feet
I can go anywhere

I have friends
Girls and boys
Most of them do not play with toys

Brandon VanCleave
Age: 11

ANDREW

Andrew is my name.
My mom and dad are to blame!
Ray is in the middle.
I do not play the fiddle.
Baines is the last.
I run really fast.

I like to play in the leaves.
I do not have fleas.
I sleep in a bed.
Sometimes I fall on my head.

I hate mice.
I do not have lice.
I like school.
But, I would rather play in a pool.

Andrew Baines
Age: 11

CATS

Cats, they leap
Cats, they jump
Cats, they pounce
they use every ounce.

Cats, they purr
while you pet
but they hate the wet.

John Holliday
Age: 11

BIRDS

Gliding through the light blue sky,
They're always by each other's side.
Wing as long as their body,
With a beak that catches the moon,
What is this animal?

Just about always see them in the sky,
They catch fish with their claws,
Not all of them have claws you see,
Feathers in the sky.
The animal may be a bird or it maybe could be me.

Hollie Pratt
Age: 11

FALL

Fall! Fall! I love fall
Because it's the time to play basketball.

When I walk outside I feel the breeze
blow through my hair, I wonder if fall is here.

But when I go out in the night air,
I see all the leaves falling off the trees.
Then I know fall is here.

I love when I stand on the porch
on a moonlit sky of fall.

Brad Ratliff
Age: 10

God is so good
God is so great
So love Him always
and don't hate
but if you do
He will forgive you
because He is our faith

Brittney Hayden
Age: 10

AUTUMN

Autumn is the time of the year
when the leaves fall off of the trees.

It is the time of the year
to rake leaves up into big fluffy piles.

Autumn is the time of the year
when the leaves change colors,
red, orange, green, yellow and brown.

The colors are so pretty.
The colors are all around.

Elizabeth Lynn Slone
Age: 9

FALL IS WONDERFUL

Fall is a beautiful time of year,
You may see a lot of deer.
Fall has lots of pretty leaves,
We have to wear long sleeves.
Fall is the time to trick-or-treat,
People give out candy for us to eat.
So fall is my favorite season,
For some unknown reason.

Justin Millay
Age: 9

MY PUMPKIN

I got a pumpkin in the fall,
I picked the best one of all.

It weighed about fifty pounds,
Fifty pounds and about one ounce.

I took it home and carved its mouth,
And then I took all the seeds out.

Next I carved its eyes and nose,
I almost dropped it on my toes.

I put it in the windowsill,
Then I heard a little girl squeal.

That night when it was very dark,
I lit a candle with a spark.

It glowed so very very bright,
During that very long night.

It glowed so bright like a light,
It looked so pretty on that night.

Nathan Mills
Age: 10

THE MORNING OF THANKSGIVING

The morning of Thanksgiving
and all through the house,
The smell could even entice a mouse.

I woke up from my sleep to see
where the smell came from,
Through the door the relatives come.

Mom was slapping hands as they
all tried to sneak a bite,
She said "That isn't very polite!"

The cousins were watching the parade
in the living room,
While all the dads were being chased
from the kitchen with a broom.

I hardly couldn't wait to eat,
And when I got to the table there was no seat.

I told my mom to fill up my plate,
I sat in the floor and that's where I ate.

The food was so good it didn't matter where I sat,
I even shared a piece of turkey with the cat.

With my belly full I fell fast to sleep,
In my dreams I counted turkey instead of sheep.

Heather Coleman

OH MAN

Oh man oh man
If maybe so
Or flounder flounder
In the sea...
Such a tiresome life
I got for me
Once more.
I love her dear
For all my life...

Bobby Dean Bowling
Age: 12

I can't go out,
When the wind is about.
Halloween is scary,
But Thanksgiving is merry.
The leaves are falling from the trees,
Pretty colors up to my knees.
Apples, picnics, and pumpkins all,
These are the merry things of fall.

Casey Duckwall
Age: 9

SLEEPY NIGHT

The stars are twinkling
The moon is shining bright
It gives me a funny feeling
That you will sleep tonight

Laura Harrison
Age: 10

FALL

The leaves are crackling beneath my feet,
They seem to dance to a steady beat.

Around and around they fly,
While the wind comes whizzing by.

I'm wearing a sweater because it's turning cold,
The season after spring is still on hold.

I make big leaf piles they are fun,
I'm glad fall is here because fall is fun.

Renee Thompson
Age: 9

REMEMBER

I know we'll meet again,
no matter the distance between.
Remembering the, "good old times"
the memories we've seen.
Others will come and go,
leaving laughter and tears.
Thinking of the past times,
now called "wonder years."
But I know you cannot hide,
the feelings of "remember when,"
Just keep my love in your heart,
for advice now and then.
Now school days are forgotten,
a new life now begins.
With brand-new "remember whens."
Don't' ever lose your goals my friend,
Don't turn your heart away,
for when you open your eyes.
I'll be there for you each day.

Alishia Rae Combs
Age: 13

RING

I had a little dog its name was Ring
Around its nose I tied a string
I pulled the string
And his nose turned blue
Get away little Ring I'm through with you

Clinton Alexander Stacy
Age: 13

WINTER

Wintertime is almost here
And when it comes I'll have no fear.
I'm ready for the snow to fall
As I hear my mother's soft call.
Put on your coats and gloves today
We'll go outside right away.
We'll build a snowman big and tall
And watch the children as they fall.
I'll throw snowballs at my friends
Today as we have lots of fun on a snowy day.
I hope it snows a lot this year
'Cause I'm going to enjoy it without any fear...

Tara LaShea Pauley

I'D MUCH RATHER

I'd much rather drink from a flowing stream
than from a kitchen faucet.
I'd much rather use the light of the sun
than the light from a lamp.
I'd much rather hear the sounds of birds chirping
than the sound of a blasting stereo.
I'd much rather be poor and happy
than rich and sad.
I'd much rather be me
than someone they all want me to be.
I'd much rather be your love
than your friend.
I'd much rather be your friend
than your nobody.
I'd much rather be with you right now
that writing this poem.

Rebecca Jones
Age: 12

LIFE

Life is precious for those that know.
Life is hope for those who care.
When the end is near, the sign will show.
Life is over when there's no one there.

The memories, the tears.
They all come back.
You think of all the years.
And all the pain your heart can pack.

So think of that when you don't care.
Think of all the good times and the bad.
Think of life when you wish you weren't there.
Think of your life when you're down and sad.

Think of others that have lost their life.
Think of your best friend going away.
Think of that before another fight.
Think of this every day.

Kayla Mosley
Age: 13

BEST FRIEND

Blue eyes like the ocean.
Skin like the snow.
Leaves falling slowly in the wind
makes me think of my brown-haired friend.

All the times she stood by me,
makes me feel like there's nobody like my friend,
to the top of the tallest mountain
to the bottom of the deepest sea.
My friend stood by me.

Even though we will one day say good-bye.
We will be together until the day I die.

Regina Yvette Smith
Age: 12

FALL

Deer season is in: poor deer -- poor deer
I wonder if the girls will miss their male deer
I hope the fawns aren't too worried
because their dads will be back in a hurry.

Whitney Crews
Age: 11

HALLOWEEN

a frightful night which is a sight
cats will turn black
witches come out and see about a little boy
there's supernatural all around
then he starts to hear a sound
he runs and screams and tries to hide
the sun comes up they disappear
he waits again to next year

Shane Edward Terry
Age: 11

AUTUMN

When it turns cool that is the sign
Autumn is here and it is time,
Time for sweaters, time for leaves
Falling off with the gentle breeze.

They turn different colors, red, yellow, brown,
I wonder what they look like in some other town.

I make big leaf piles, they are fun
Everybody jumps in I'm not the only one,
Autumn now is much fun
I'm glad it is here to follow the sun.

Jennifer Bellamy
Age: 9

SNOWBALLS

We had a cat that was white
he had the fleas and ate mice
one mouse he ate gave him the tummyache

Sandra Marie Sturgill
Age: 11

FRIENDS

Friends,
friends are special people,
who are there to help you
in the time of need.

Friends are people
who you can share
your feelings with when
you're feeling incomplete.

Friends are always there
to make your life better when
no one else is there.

Always in life you'll
have a special person
who'll always stick around.

Heather Williams
Age: 11

WOULD A TREE MAKE A SOUND?

If a big tree fell
And nobody was around
Would it make a sound?

Ben T. Hodson
Age: 10

THE BIG, FAT JOLLY MAN

At this special time of year,
when everyone's spreading Christmas cheer.

There's only one man in charge,
You might say he's rather large.

He's got a snowy, white beard that's oh so long,
Ho, ho, ho, is his holiday song.

He rides around in his shiny sleigh,
You won't catch him out during the day.

We leave him cookies on Christmas Eve,
No, I'm not talking about a man named Steve.

With a sack of toys and on occasion, some snowballs,
He's the big, fat jolly man named
Santa Claus!

Justin Wells
Age: 9

HOG WILD

Hog wild runs like fire
Jumps in the air and says I don't care
Hog wild running through the night

Snorty, nasty things rolling in the mud
Jumps up in the air again and says...
Hey! I eat crud
Hog wild running through the night

Running, running hits a block of coal
And says I'll call Joel at the poll
A hog out of a whole company
Hog wild running through the night

It's nighttime, it's nighttime, he can't see,
He trips, he falls and gets his head stuck in a tree
Hog wild running through the night

He's sliding on ice, he's sliding on ice,
He trips and falls on his big fat ugly face
Hog wild running through the night

Justin Noble
Age: 11

HOW TO GO AROUND A CORNER

Corners
   are
     the places
      where
streets run down to meet

     Corners
      are
       surprises
        on almost any street

       At
        almost
         any corner
          it's better to wait

        And
         turn
          the corner
          slowly
           as if it was a gate

Christa Mosley
Age: 11

TOY STORE

I like the toy store it really rules
Aisles of toys are really cool

Toys as far as you can see
All waiting there for little old me

So many toys it's hard to choose
I'll take them all so I can't lose

Emily Rose
Age: 11

CHRISTMAS

Christmas is joyful
Christmas is jolly
Christmas is when
We gather the holly

Christmas is fun
Because of the gifts
Especially the one
Named Jesus the son

Christmas is over
Too quickly you see but
There's always next year
For gifts and a tree

Amber C. Little
Age: 11

A LITTLE CROCUS, A LITTLE HOPE

Working in front of Cushing Hall,
I found a small purple flower that was so beautiful,
Growing on the ground.

Without thinking,
I plucked the little flower and ran to my mom,
With it clutched, in my little hand.
"Oh, Mom," I cried,
Jumping up and down.
"I'm taking this, home to Dad."
"This will surely make him feel better and not be so sad."

If, just looking at it, made me feel so glad,
Maybe holding it in his hurt hand,
I could get back the father, I once had.

But Mom softly, explained about the now fading bloom.
It was only meant, to brighten the outside gloom.
We went outside together
And looked at the tiny flowers.

Standing so gaily and still,
Mom said though, Crocus were from God.
It would take God's will
For Daddy to heal.

So maybe, I'll just tell Dad
About the pretty crocus, instead.
As tonight, I kneel in prayer, by his bed.

Jessicca Slone
Age: 10

TURKEY DAY

Gobble gobble goes the turkey,
His meat tastes better than beef jerky.

Gobble gobble there he goes again,
Strutting around his smelly pen.

Gobble gobble we don't hear,
Poor little bird was quite a dear!!

Matthew F. Perez
Age: 9

CHRISTMAS

Christmas is a holiday that is a birthday.
A birthday that is special.
The birthday of the Lord.
The Lord called Jesus.
On Christmas, Jesus gives up his presents
and gives them to the children of earth.
Christmas is also the time you need to be jolly
for old Saint Nick comes and flies
around the earth in one night!
So good night to all that know this.

Daniel Lee Gibbins
Age: 10

HALLOWEEN

Halloween, Halloween, oh what a fright,
Will zombies and ghosts take a big bite,
Help! Help! The mummy is trying to steal,
A jewel that is very real.
Let's don't let them get away.
Let's make him mad and make him pay!

Ashley E. Keller
Age: 8

CHRISTMAS

At Christmastime
Snowflakes twinkle, shimmer, and shine.

All the people are at the store,
spending all their money until they're poor.
Oh well, what's money for
if you can't buy presents that people adore?

We see smiling faces all about
just waiting for presents to be handed out.
Goodies and treats, we're looking forward to,
happily singing the whole season through.
Boy, oh boy, I bet I gained a pound or two,
from all that good food. How about you?

Ashley Warnock
Age: 10

THANKSGIVING

Thanksgiving is a wonderful day
We celebrate it in a big way
Lots of food and fun
Always something for everyone
Turkey, dressing, cranberry sauce
Horseshoes, darts, and ring toss
Thanksgiving to me is a special day
Because I know Christmas is the next holiday

Amber Gail Beasley
Age: 8

THANKSGIVING IS...

Thanksgiving is...
Thanking God for this wonderful day.
Thanksgiving is...
Having all your family with you.
Thanksgiving is...
Fun and friendship for everyone.
Thanksgiving is not only a day to eat,
it's a day to enjoy and be with your family and friends.

Christen P. Coleman

BETTER OFF

I know we feel deep sorrow,
I know we feel great pain.
Without Him on this earth,
Life just won't be the same!
He has begun a new life,
A life with no more pain,
For of the name of Jesus Christ,
He never was ashamed!
He has a place in Heaven
Far beyond the sky.
A place where joy shall never end
And tears shall dim no eye.
Now he's walking on streets of gold
Beside the crystal sea.
He's so much better than you and I
On this earth could ever be.

In loving memory
1997

Jenny Thomas
Age: 14

FLOWERS IN THE WOODS

Daucus caruta, so dainty and white,
The bug in the middle is quite a sight.
Taken home to your mother and put in a vase,
She'll say, "Oh, look at the lovely Queen Anne's Lace."

Cirsium vulgare, so sharp and blue,
Round at the top and prickly, too.
Watch when your friends give a whistle,
Or you might run into this thistle.

Solidago rigosa, so bright and yellow,
It's the flower of Kentucky that's soft and mellow.
You can find the root deep in the sod,
Pull it up and you have Goldenrod.

Aster linariifolius, which shows up in the fall,
Orange, red, yellow, both large and small.
In a flower bed or a beautiful bouquet,
I'll choose the aster any day.

Trifolium pratense, some would call a weed,
To a horse or hare however, it's considered feed.
This worldly wild flower grows all over,
Man and horse call it Red Clover.

Bidens aristasa, bright and yellow,
This is a snack shop for a sparrow.
In the grass this plant may cower,
It is called the Tickseed Sunflower.

Impatiens capensis, the flower that says, "No,"
It closes up if too near you go.
This plant is named a Spotted Touch-me-not,
They are just wonderful in a flowerpot.

Heather D. Lucas
Age: 10

Preacher, referee, umpire, Dad,
he also treats cancer, for people who are sad,
he tries to make his patients glad,
he really is the greatest DAD.
He has two pretty daughters and a wife,
what else can you ask for in this life?
He works very hard and is also funny,
whenever he's not working
he's at Murray State running.
As you can see he has no spare time,
but he's the greatest DAD and I'm proud that he's mine.

Brittany Kay Miles
Age: 11

HALLOWEEN

Halloween, Halloween, what a fright.
It happened one very scary night.
Halloween, Halloween, oh those mummies.
They act so silly, like a bunch of dummies.

Justin DeJarnatt
Age: 8

On turkey day we played a game of guessing.
Then we sat and had turkey and dressing.
We ate lots and lots of that turkey.
Mom saved a leg just for me.
After eating I'm not hungry anymore,
Then we leave and walk out the door.

Jackie Franklin
Age: 8

WHAT I SEE

You say they are so different,
But still they're really the same;
Why can't you stop this mess
And call them by their names?

People are always people;
Are you too blind to see
All the pain that you can cause,
Not just to them, but to me?

I'm sorry for my family,
But he is the one I love;
I honestly feel that God
Has sent him from above.

Why can't you accept my feelings
And see him for who he is?
Why can't you be happy for me,
And know I want this to be?

He may be a different color,
But that doesn't matter to me;
What's important is on the inside,
And that is what I see.

Cathy Zalucki
Age: 15

FEAR

Though fear is felt by every person
I find it captivating, mysterious,
interesting and even intriguing.
So powerful and yet
we can't pinpoint it to just one thing.

Why is that? Why isn't there just one fear?
Could it be that fear is an illusion?
I think not!
Fear is very real, it's often
making people go crazy or scared to live.

Why do we let fear dangle us from a string
and violently jerk us around
until it triumphantly conquers us?
Why don't we capture it and bury it
in the depths of the earth?

Why? I'll tell you why.
Fear can't be overthrown by anyone or anything.
And besides, there are people like me
who find it captivating, and intriguing!
Does that scare you? It should!

Rebekah Ellen Perkins
Age: 15

THE LIGHT

My mother answers the phone
So late at night
I listen to every word she says
Wait for her to hang up
See the tears in her eyes
Hear the disappointment in her voice
Watch her head drop as if embarrassed
Hear the dreadful news
Think how could this happen
Wonder what the future holds
Hope for the best outcome possible

We never expect it
But unwelcomed news does and will arrive
When we least suspect it
That one call or knock will invade
Our peaceful existence
Still whatever the trouble
We have to look towards the future
Pray for the best and stay calm
That's the only way we'll
See the light through the darkest times

Casey Jo Humphreys
Age: 15

TO LIVE AND DIE BY THE SWORD

There once was a knight that roamed the land,
he was the most valiant and mighty man.
He bravely fought in every war,
returning hither with very few sores.
His squire was a knave that despised him so,
that he plotted the death of this mighty hero.
As the knight donned his armor for battle one day,
he felt a prick in his neck, then staggered, then swayed.
He had fallen prey to a poison-tipped tack,
which dug even deeper as he lie on his back.
The knave looked on in utter content,
a smile crossed his face for the knight was spent.
Then came the others that would fight this day,
they mourned for the knight as he lie in the way.
Then they reasoned that the knave should replace,
the honorable knight that lie dead on his face.
They stripped the knight of his armor
And began to donn,
the knave resisted heavily but still they worked on.
They dressed him completely except for the helm,
inside which the poison-tipped nail was held.
They placed it on him with a few friendly pats,
then the knave swayed a bit and fully collapsed.
This is the moral of all these lines,
control your envy if you value your lives.
It's dangerous when envy turns to revenge instead,
you could ask the knave but he's already dead.

Raven Nicole Shelton
Age: 15

Happy New Year, it's January you know
  A month with still a lot of snow.
Now it's the month with lots of love,
  February with a beautiful sky above.
The flowers have begun to bloom
  It's March I will assume.
April brings yet more flowers,
  And there's always an abundance of
  Warm spring showers.
May is the month of graduation,
  And preparation for summer vacation.
Wedding bells in June do ring,
  Swimming is my favorite thing.
It's really hot in July,
  When fireworks light up the sky.
Vacations are over, and it was so cool,
  But August is here and it's time for school.
It's my friend's birthday in September,
  She thinks I'll forget, but I'll always remember.
In October the leaves start falling,
  Soon the ghosts and goblins will be calling.
We get to eat in November,
  Because the pilgrims we remember.
It's December and the year has past,
  Yeah, it's Christmastime at last.

Lynise Allison McMackin
Age: 12

IN THE SKY ON AIR

In the sky on air;
In the sky on air;
In the sky on air;
No, it's on a swing...
But it doesn't matter;
'Cause when you're on a swing,
And when you close your eyes,
It FEELS...
Like you're flying in the sky.

Tyler Elizabeth Spann
Age: 5

I love Thanksgiving day
It is special in every-way
We go to Granny's
Then we end up at Nanny's
We eat turkey
Then I'll get perky.
We make a lot of noise
When we play with all our toys
After that my brother hunts for deer
I hope they stay near
"I do like pumpkin pie,"
I said with a sigh.
I also said "Dig in let's eat!"
Nanny said "Be neat be neat!"

Amber Thomas

STOP AND SMELL THE ROSES

Walking down the road one day,
As I often do,
I realized there were things around,
Things that changed my view.

I never noticed this before,
Why was it suddenly so clear?
And then I heard a voice inside,
"My child, do not fear."

I walked a little farther,
Still peering on novel things,
Time seemed to pass so rapidly,
Like the beating of hummingbird wings.

I was surrounded by awesome beauty,
All that one's life could behold.
Now I know to "stop and smell the roses"
Without having to be told.

Life can get really hectic,
And most of the time we don't slow down
Then we look back and wish we'd paid attention
To all the sights and sounds.

So stop and smell the roses,
Take all the time one needs,
Just be sure when God calls you home,
You have done your deeds.

Melissa Jackson
Age: 15

A CAT WHO ALWAYS LIKED TO SCAT

Did you ever see,
a cat who always liked to scat?
If you never saw,
a cat who always liked to scat,
you should buy a cat,
to see a cat scat.
If you can't buy a cat,
to see a cat scat,
I will tell you,
how a cat scats.
Your cat will always go out the back door,
when you're sleeping in your bed-o.
One day you'll hear some,
garbage cans clanging,
and you may wonder,
what has happened.
But I can tell you right now,
this minute that,
it was a cat,
who always liked to scat.
That is how,
a real cat scats.

Damir Kusmic
Age: 10

COLORS

Colors are beautiful from red to green.
Even underneath the blue sky's scene
Colors live on purple kites.
They also live on the silvery moonlight!
When the sun wakes up at dawn
You can see the rich green lawn.
Let your creative minds flow,
To where the yellow stars glow!
Colors make the world go 'round
From bright pink to dark brown!

Jessica Martin
Age: 11

I'll be back you'd better be sitting
Kayla, Marsha quit hitting
Brian, Sean quit playing games
Crystal you may take names
Jacob, Justin don't lean back in your chair
Leeann I love your hair!
Matt please start your writing
Andrew stop fighting
Josh quit walking
Bobby stop talking
Laura and Renee are the last of the crew
except for Mrs. Goins and me too!

Alecia Bachuss

ONE FINE DAY

Have you ever looked at the clouds on a beautiful day?
Have you ever picked clovers and just wanted to play?
Have you ever watched beautiful birds fly by?
Have you ever rubbed your feet
In the grass and sighed?

One day you should lie out and bathe in the sun.
One day you should let it all out and have some fun.
You shouldn't get wrapped up in what you do.
You should go look at the world anew.

The world is something that you shouldn't waste
Get out and do something now -- post haste!
Love the world and everything,
Be it hand, claw, hoof, or wing.

Brandon Simpson
Age: 13

THANKSGIVING DAY

It is Thanksgiving day.
I wake up and pray.
I go outside and play.
I like to play all day.
Our dad gets us a turkey to eat.
When we are done we are very sweet.

David Ray Cary

LOST ON THE STREETS

He's Changing

He's following the wrong crowd.
He's really confused about what he wants to do.
He doesn't even know who he is anymore.

He's Lost

He's not the same person he was before.
He took the blame, now he's in shame.

He's Changing

Crystal Cassady
Age: 14

You are special
In so many ways
You are special
All through the days

You are special
In Mother's eyes
You are special
Even in mine.

Dustie Dawn McDowell
Age: 12

THE ROAD OF LIFE

The road of life, twisted and curved
Taking the wrong path, feeling disturbed
Yielding for death and sad memories we share
Analyzing a fork or signs that say
Beware!

Slowing at a speed bump for age
Like a book of life trying to turn the next page
Speeding through in times with our friends
Sometimes choosing the wrong road
And coming to an end.

Stopping and going through good times and bad
Hitting a bump that makes you feel sad
So many choices, we must pass through strife
Never knowing on
the Road of Life.

Caitlin Marie McGill
Age: 12

BULL

I am a bull
see my big horns
attacking for food
mean.

Deborah Keller
Age: 9

SOARING FREE

I am the eagle soaring free.
Over the mountains above the trees.

I soar over Indians dancing and praying to me.
From around a fire in the trees.

I will set their tortured spirits free.
Take them to the great beyond to live in eternal peace.

I am the eagle soaring free I shall set their spirits free.
So they may soar alongside of me.

Yes, I am the eagle soaring free
I shall set their spirits free.
So they may soar alongside of me.

Mark E. Green
Age: 13

HALLOWEEN

Halloween, Halloween, oh what a fright,
I saw a ghost it was white like a flying kite,
He might even bite me.
Watch out I can't see,
Oops, I just hit a tree!

Savara Tolbird
Age: 8

THE SACRIFICE

Magnificent oak tree
Standing tall
Over the man with the shining blade
Yelling as the tree falls

Tree resting on pallets in the lumberyard store
Homeless man buys its untreated wood
Builds a small hut
And is saved by the tree
    Which remains
Years after the man is gone
Falling and crumbling

    The tree is left

for poor children to crawl to its shelter
    nearly numb from the coldness they strike a match
And the tree knows

its end has come to a burning
    warmth of flame
    the magnificent tree
    standing tall
    gives its life proudly
    to the children

who survive another night

Benjamin David Hays
Age: 13

JACKSON

Fluffy ears, puffy tail,
describe you Jackson,
you'll never fail.
You love to play and sit and cuddle,
you love your bed in which you snuggle.
You love your ball that used to squeak,
in every-way you are unique.
You love to crunch and munch on ice,
you're always filled with pep and spice.
You are the only dog for me.
I hope that this will always be.

Your puffy tail wags in delight,
your smile widens at the sight.
Of squirrels chasing in the trees,
and butterflies and bumblebees.
You bark, you whine, you scratch the door,
you urge me to let you go explore.
And when I finally let you out,
you leap and run and hop about.

And when it's time to come back in,
you scratch the back door once again.
I hear you whine and bark so loud,
but Jackson you make me so very proud.
I'm glad you are always there for me,
because of you I'm filled with glee...

Lindsay Marie Bettermann
Age: 11

DOES HE LOVE ME?

There's a white little frog, that stares every day.
He swims in my tank, in his own little way.
Does he love me?

Does he love me or despise?
When he looks at me, with his big, black, eyes.
He swims, then stares, then gives me a glare.
How can I tell him, it's for his own good?
Should I let him be free?
Does he love me?

I can tell he is happy, by the way he smiles,
with no teeth in his mouth.
I know he is happy, in his four-walled, glass house.
I know he loves me, as well as me him.
Then I'll watch him swim, again and again.
I look in his tank, and I walk away.
Yet, he still stares, day after day.
Yes he loves me!

Tiffany Hamilton
Age: 12

BASKETBALL

A sport, not just any sport,
A sport of life,
A sport with the cutting edge.
Basketball it's a sport.

Michael Reed Hamilton
Age: 11

THANKSGIVING DAY

A day that Pilgrims and Indians joined together,
and feasted and talked like brothers and sisters.
A day to be happy for good living,
and to share with others through giving.
So on this day we eat turkey and dressing,
and we thank God for the year's blessing.

Natalie Wilson

TIME

Time, slips through your fingers
Time, it flies away, flashing by as it goes.
Time is a great power,
Time cannot be controlled,
Time just melts away,
Time waits for no man,
So use your time carefully and wisely,
Or time will pass you by.

Eric Sanders
Age: 13

FRIEND

Up on a mountain,
  High in the trees,
    One man, one woman grieve

The loss of a friend.
  His life now ends.
    His spirit soars into the sky,
      He becomes a beautiful butterfly.

The firelight warms.
  Weep no more, for he is reborn,
    And will return once again.
      Our brave, true friend.

Allen C. Wade Jr.
Age: 13

THE GHOST OF LOST RIVER CAVE

I am a ghost,
  white and scary
I haunt the Lost River Cave
  to scare away trespassers
    onto the
      Lost River Cave property.

I am a ghost,
  white and scary,
I have been here over a hundred years.
  I guard the treasure of
    Jessie James

I am a ghost,
  white and scary,
I dance to the music
  coming from the band on the stage
    at the Lost River Cave nightclub.

I am a ghost,
  white and scary,
I hide in the cave
  and when you go past me
    I will come up behind
      and whisper in your ear...

GET OUT OF MY CAVE!!!!!

Joseph Lyle Harris
Age: 12

CLOSING IN

The jungle is thick,
My heart is pumping,
My muscles tense,
In an instant my life can end,
Will I meet an enemy or a friend?
Will my destiny be to die?
Never again to see my kids and wife,
A soldier's ultimate sacrifice.

These many thoughts roll inside my brain,
Then my squad partner cries out in pain,
As my tears start to roll,
A terrible rage comes over my soul,
I threw my gun up and fired a round,
To let them know I'm standing my ground
Then something hit me,
Blood fell like rain,
Blackness took over,
I no longer felt pain.

Cheyenne Click
Age: 13

DANCE TAP

Dancing tap is an enjoyable and wonderful sport.
It doesn't matter if you're tall or short.
Dancing tap takes hard work, practice, and effort too,
and you have magic silver taps
on the bottom of your shoe.
You practice and practice for that one big thing.
You think you're ready when
your stomach begins to sing!
As you go out on that mammoth stage,
you feel free as a bird out of its cage.
You do your best and dance your fluttering heart out,
then the audience loudly claps and begins to shout!
At that moment I suddenly realize
that I'm truly a dancer in everyone's eyes.
After the lights dim, and my shoe makes
its last and final clack,
I'm ready to go home and happily hit the sack.

Abby Grow

DID YOU EVER WONDER.....

As I stared clueless into the TV,
the load of What if's dashed as fast as the eye can see,
into my brain through the mess it contained,
to boggle, to worry, to terrorize, to remain.

What if my parents come down with the flu?
What if my friend moves away to Perdue?
What if my cat won't come down from the tree?
What if the dinos come back from B.C.?
What if a tornado picks me up off my feet?
What if I drown in polluted Drakes Creek?
What if our neighborhood's taken over by E.T.?
What if on my report card I notice a D?
What if the rain won't leave us alone?
What if I leave my homework at home?
What if Chipper Jones decides to retire?
What if my house catches on fire?
What if I'm kidnapped by someone I don't know?
What if I'm paralyzed from head to toe?
What if I have a wreck and die?
What if the deer tell Kentucky good-bye?
What if my house disappears into thin air?
What if I become ill, and no one seems to care?
What if my dog is found dead in the road?
What if a hurricane whips through
   and takes with it a load?

The What if's leaped away thrilled
that they changed my life,
And I sat in amazement knowing I'd soon live in strife,
On the edge of my seat, until I die,
Hoping none of these wonders would become live,

In my life I worry enough already,
I just can't take more than the load I previously carry.

Lauren Phillips
Age: 12

CHANGE

Change will come
      Change is here
            Love fades out
                 Then love appears

Now my water's turned to wine
And these thoughts I have,
I claim as mine.

Change has been
      Change will be
            Time will tell
                 Time will ease.

Now my curtain has been drawn
And my heart is free to go,
But where does my heart belong?

Jenny Singleton
Age: 14

BLUE IS

Blue is.....the sky looking down anxiously
at the world.

It is Wildcat uniforms hanging peacefully
in the locker before the game.

It is eyes looking furiously
at my mean brother.

It is taffy hanging scrumptiously
on the rack at the candy store.

It is shirts lying placidly
in a drawer.

It is water flowing calmly
down the river.

Kristi Henderson
Age: 9

TURKEY

There was an old turkey that had an old wobble
He got it when he tried to gobble
He fell off an old log
There was a lot of fog
That's why today he hobbles

Brittany Shown
Age: 11

The apple was eating
a worm ----
I said,
"Why are you eating a worm?"
"I like it"
said the apple.
"I don't"
said the worm.

Stephanie Evans
Age: 6

THE DANCING SUN

Across the barren wastelands
By the primitive pyramids of Egypt
A spirited, young woman glides across the sands
Her long, flowing hair cascading to her waist
A snowy white veil drawn across her lovely face
A long, golden gown swirled around her ankles
Its golden, metallic coins, glitter and jangle
She advances, but her feet do not touch the sand
She glides and dances towards the horizon
And in an instant, she is gone
She disappears beneath the sand,
There is only the sounds of night
She will not return 'til the first signs of light

Mackenzie Maggie Duff
Age: 13

SUMMER IS...

Summer is tulips holding their heads up to the sky
Summer is flying a kite up so very high

Summer is watching rain drizzle down a windowpane
Summer is not being able to remove
    the green grass stain

Summer is the feeling of hope as you hold a fishing pole
Summer is collecting change for the roads with a toll

Summer is sipping lemonade on a hot day
Summer is the last day of vacation
    and you beg your parents to stay

Summer is the sweet smell of flowers in the air
Summer is the sight of a mother bear
    protecting her baby bear

Summer is the sunshine beating down on my face
Summer is on a hot day participating in a race

Summer is many, many things, I have just named a few
Summer is always every year new!

Ashley Parsly

ZABBA THE TUTT

The baddest maddest monster crimelord of all
Is Zabba the Tutt who's four meters wide
And two meters tall
He has a big fat belly
That shakes when he laughs like a bowl full of jelly.
He has big long fingernails and toenails
That are like claws
That he likes to use when he mauls.
His ears are wide and long
That he uses to listen to his favorite songs.
Watch out for his big battle-club tail
And his sharp teeth he uses to crunch snails.
He lumbers along on two big legs
Watch out or he'll eat your chicken eggs.
He makes noises that are loud and clear
His roars can be heard from far or near.
There's a way to protect yourself from him
Just say he's not real and he'll get real slim
He'll get slimmer and slimmer you see
Until he turns into a stick and he won't bother ye.

Jake Johnston

WHAT CAN OPEN

A door can open.
A flower can bloom.
When somebody yawns, the mouth opens really wide.
A window can open, too.

A butterfly can open its wings.
A swan can open its head from its wing.

An eye can open, too.
A box can open.
An umbrella can open.
A backpack can open.

BUT the BEST open thing
  is an OPENED MIND.

Shelby Lynn Carter
Age: 6

LEAVES ARE COLORFUL

Leaves are brown,
Leaves are green,
And yellow.
Jump in the leaves,
Funny fellow!

William Ian Elliott
Age: 6

CATS

I love cats enough to see;
How much fun they are to me.
Cats are pretty, cats are nice;
Some cats love to catch mice!
Most cats eat birds and fish;
Of course we don't serve that in their dish!
Cats are good hunters when it comes to rabbit,
After a while, chasing them becomes a habit.
Cats are wonderful little pets;
But be careful now, and don't get them wet!

Julie Kate Wilson
Age: 9

SNAPPY

There once was a cat named Snappy,
But Snappy wasn't very happy.
He lived in a house filled with love and care,
But Snappy's problem was too hard to bare.
Snappy got lots of food and attention,
But it's like he was in another dimension.
He's a beautiful cat with white silky fur,
And I love to hear him meow and purr.
You may think he's ignoring you, and is a nerd,
But the truth is, he's deaf and can't hear a word.

Stephanie Burnley
Age: 11

MY FAMILY

Dad --
I'm so glad you are my dad,
You make me feel very glad,
I know that you love me,
You make that very clear to see,
I love you Dad, I hope you know,
Even when I'm mad at you, so,
I'm telling you again,
I love you Dad, I'll love you to the end.

Mommy --
I'm so glad you are my mommy,
And you really aren't a zombie,
If you were, I'd cry with fear,
But since you aren't, I cry happy tears,
I'm happy because you love me so,
And I love you, I hope you know,
I love you Mom, I love you a bunch,
And I hope by now you've gotten the hunch,
That I love you,
Without you, I'd be blue,
So Mom I hope you've gotten the hint,
That without you, in my heart, I'd have a dent.

Greg --
Greg, my brother, I'm glad you are,
Even if I sometimes wish that you were on Mars,
I love you Greg, I really do,
I'll stick to you like Crazy Glue,
I'll love you always rain, or shine,
I'll love you past the end of time.

Megan --
This is a story about me
Megan Carol Talley
I have brown hair,
And quite a few stuffed bears,
Which are all very special to me,
But none can come close to my family.

Megan Talley
Age: 11

FALL

Fall is a time for rain,
Fall is a time for leaves to come down,
Fall is when you rake the leaves up,
When it comes Thanksgiving,
It's time for a turkey,
You are around your family,
And you say, "I hope this day doesn't go away!"

But the very next day,
Is the same old, same old day,
When you're by the fire you feel a shiver,
But until fall is over,
You shall remain to do the same old thing,
And it continues to rain,
As soon as it's over,
It shall come back.

Brandon Shockley
Age: 10

FALL

The wind is softly blowing
Daddy is doing our last minute mowing
Football is getting about over
I've got to go feed my dog Rover.
As I play in the leaves on the ground
I know there are more spreading all around
   I love fall
Yet I hate to rake the leaves that's all
As I sit on the front porch what do I see
A field full of deer looking at me!!

Vanessa J. Fields
Age: 11

AUTUMN'S FALL

As the days get cooler;
and the wind blows harder;
I can soon smell the autumn's fall.

When the leaves change color;
and the sky gets duller;
I can soon smell the autumn's fall.

As the days get shorter and nights grow longer;
I can feel the days as they get colder;
So I know autumn's fall is finally here.

Joshua Dale Finn Cogar
Age: 12

A SEASON LOVED BY MANY

Autumn is a season loved by many
The season when...
Leaves cover the cold grounds,
Giving them a touch of color.
When...
Rosy-cheeked children,
Bundle up in warm clothing to go...
Wondering through the blowing meadows.
When...
The scent of Mama's apple pie...
Tickles the tips of the children's noses,
Causing them to come back in.
When...
Papa can sit on the front porch,
Looking up from his newspaper...
To see a flock of one thousand blackbirds fly by.
When...
Billy Joe fills with excitement...
As he fills a strong tug at his line,
When he pulls he can see the large fish at his hook.
When...
A golden ray of sunlight...
Shows past the bare trees
And over the hills.

Now the season loved by many...
Has come and gone again.
For now specks of white...
Begin to fall to the grounds.

Aleia D. Shirley
Age: 11

NATURE IN THE FALL

Fall is a time of year
When people go see football games and cheer

Different colored leaves fall all around
People rake them into piles on the ground

Fall is so beautiful
Warm clothes are suitable

Sometimes snow falls from the air
Stay inside where it is warm and take care

In the fall, we set back our clock
If they don't, we won't meet our friend around the block

In the fall the wind does blow
And scatters leaves along the path we go

People go hunting for deer
Some don't even know when one comes near

Jacob Myatt
Age: 11

OUTER SPACE THINGS

Have you ever seen a thing here from outer space?
One with big eyes and an ugly green face!
Have you ever seen a thing land here from Pluto?
He crash-landed in a U.F.O.
Have you ever seen a thing land here from Neptune?
He's scheduled to arrive here very, very soon!
Have you ever seen a thing with a Uranus license plate?
His mouth moves at a constant rate!
Have you ever seen a Saturn thing?
They wear a million dollar ring!
Have you ever seen a thing called "Jupiter Fella?"
In fear of the Red Storm they carry an umbrella!
Have you ever seen a thing land here from Mars?
He has a certain craving for candy bars!
Have you ever seen a thing here from Venus?
He's really, really smart like an earthling genius!
Have you ever seen a thing with Mercury as its
Home planet?
If he sees something he really, really wants
He'll all at once can it!
I've never seen a thing from outer space,
That would definitely put a smile on my face!

Hillary Johnson

THE ROSE

There once was a beautiful full bloomed rose
It was the most beautiful thing I had seen
It was standing there like a big beautiful light beam.

It had stood out to me like the sun
But it had just begun!!!!!

I picked it up and was walking home,
then I heard Mama say dinner's ready so
come, come, come!

When I got home, I put it in a vase
with some water.

Then I hurried off to school,
But as soon as I got there, I felt like a fool.

I shouldn't have left it alone,
so I hurried home.

When I got home I saw the most saddest thing.
It had passed away.

So I took it outside and laid it on the ground,
just like I had found.

That poor little rose that once was beautiful,
had faded away in the evening dew.

Kristen Blick
Age: 13

FALL, FALL

Leaves with color
fall to the ground,
a beautiful sight,
all around.
The wind blows gently
the birds always sing,
to make my mind wander,
from everything.
See the children warmly dressed,
ready to go out and play,
and turn a very quiet morning,
into a special fall day.
We will take advantage of fall
because it won't last very long,
and when it's time
for the season to go away
we'll whisper softly,
come back fall, visit someday!

Marie Witty
Age: 11

THANKSGIVING

T hanks we give on this day,
H ave you eaten yet?
A ll come to eat.
N othing left on the table.
K eep your jacket on when you're outside.
S upper's over now.
G o and get the dessert.
I 'm stuffed.
V ery stuffed I am.
I want to go play.
N ot now.
G ive thanks first.

Kelli Woodward
Age: 10

DAWN OF ANGER

ANGER...the horror lurking within
    every human being on the earth.

ANGER...a human volcano ready to erupt
    with the slightest touch.

ANGER...steaming lava from the human volcano,
    destroying everything in its path.

ANGER...chaos spreading its virus worldwide.

ANGER...origin of earth's wars.

ANGER...a brush fire casting its flaming red
    and orange fire across the world.

ANGER...burns through millions of souls every day
    like fire burning paper.

ANGER...a split-second strike that causes
    destruction to the heart.

ANGER...a fully loaded weapon ready to fire
    with the single pull of a trigger.

ANGER...crushes goodness like a tiny bug
underneath an enormous foot.

Only one person can defeat the monster within...

YOU...YOU...YOU!

Joshua Tyler London
Age: 10

CHRISTMAS MORNING

I lie in my bed thinking,
counting the minutes.
My parents call us out.
(I thought they never would!)
"Time to open presents!" says Mother.
We stare with twinkling eyes at all the presents.
I open a present.
"Wow! A castle!" I yell.
After we open presents, we jump into a pile
of ribbons and get all tangled up.
A child's delight on Christmas morning.

Katie Shoemaker
Age: 10

SWIMMING

S plishing and splashing.
W ater everywhere you look.
I nto the pool!
M y dad can do a cannon ball.
M y dad is great at swimming.
I nto a towel.
N ever run on the side of the pool.
G etting to swim.

James Michael Berry II
Age: 9

HALLOWEEN

Witches and ghosts all around
then they all make a gruesome sound

Wolves howl deep in the night
and the air fills with screams of fright

Then the wind makes a sound
and cracks of thunder shake the ground

All the children run back in
and sort their candy with a grin

When all the witches have gone away
and it's the beginning of another day

Then normal people fill the streets
and there's no more scaring for many weeks

And when Halloween comes back again
I'll be sure to wear a grin!

Amanda Rasnic
Age: 10

ANDREW SNOW

Once there was a boy named Andrew Snow
Whose attitude was very very low
He sat on his couch all day long
Never even trying with other people to get along
Watching TV was what he liked to do
He would never try things that are new
You could hear his griping from far away
Between his shoulders is where his head would lay
One day he decided to go out that door
To see out there what lied in store
He walked right down to the b-ball floor
Just to be walking and nothing more
About that time a ball came his way
Can you give us that he heard someone say
He picked it up and threw it to the sky
As it went through the net the kids yelled oh my
From that day on he had a sport
Basketball out on that court
He was the town's Little League Star
He beat everyone else by far
So Andrew Snow got his dream
To be a somebody, shine and gleam

David Wright
Age: 13

TEDDY BEAR

Teddy bear,
Teddy bear,
Soft as can be.
As I scoop him up in my arms
He looks at me.
I love to hold him just for fun
Because he feels as warm as the sun.

When I leave home
I hate to see him alone.
I always think of taking him along
But I decide to leave him
At his home sweet home.

Priscilla Christie
Age: 11

HERSHEY'S KISS

It looks like an upside-down funnel.
It feels like a mountain melting in my mouth.
The mountain gets smaller, but the taste gets larger.
It's dark and thick.
The smell lingers as the taste fades, fades,
Fades.

Joseph Magistri

P oems
O nomatopoeias
E xciting
T hemes
R hyming
Y ear-round

Stephen William Eidson
Age: 11

FALL

Bright leaves descending.
Animals know fall has come.
Time to gather food.
For some it is time to leave,
Others will slumber and dream.

Meghan Welsh
Age: 10

BIG TREE

Big tree on the ground
Do you ever weep and frown?
Big tree up in the sky
I wonder if you ever cry
Big tree there are bats in your branches
Do you like them in your limbs?
Big tree you are my favorite tree
No tree could ever replace you
I wonder how long you will be around
And when you might fall down
Really early in the morning
The glittery dew falls on your leaves
Big tree in the sunset
I'm glad you're here.

Erika Ashley Henderson
Age: 9

HALLOWEEN NIGHT

Halloween night
Gives me a fright
The monsters, skeletons, and witches are quite a sight
The party had goodies and the goodies were good
Bigfoot had a size thirty and they fit good
Halloween night is quite a fright

Andrew Tyler Clark
Age: 9

FOUR SEASONS

First comes winter.
It starts a new year,
that is cold and breezy,
three months long.

One third of winter already past,
back in December,
where Christmas is,
and some of the snow.

Then spring comes next
and melts all the snow away.
Spring sprouts,
the leaves and flowers.

Spring grows the grass,
so we can run and play in it.
Then we can lie in it.
It warms the water, so we can swim.

The summer comes along and it gets so hot,
we have to swim in the lake.
We go boating and fishing all day long.
We can catch as many fish as we want.

Then on the Fourth of July,
we celebrate our independence.
We watch the fireworks in the sky,
looking like stars when they blow up.

Then comes autumn when
all the leaves start to fall,

and they start to change to
light green, red, orange, yellow, and brown.

It starts to get colder and colder,
so we can't swim in the lake,
all the leaves fall off the trees,
and winter comes again.

Jacie Danielle Brumitt
Age: 12

MY FAVORITE TEACHER

There was one teacher I loved most;
　　She taught me many things.
One of the things was not to boast,
　　For that I give her a toast.

She taught me to have fun in school,
　　And that doing homework is cool.
She taught me how to be a friend,
　　And to lend a helping hand.

There was one thing she taught me,
　　That I will never forget.
She taught me how to think,
　　But also how to dream.
　　For she is full of gleam;
She is Mrs. Ruth Dauley.

Whitney Eggleston

DEER

is fur
is warm
can run fast
can jump high
is pretty
when you hunt deer
sometimes you will see
sometimes you won't
you have to sit
for a long time
sometimes you don't
but if you miss a deer
you will be upset
and you will be mad
because if you shot at a deer
you will want to hit it.

Derrick Lance Markham
Age: 12

Mrs. Dauley,
She was so jolly.

She loved the Wildcats,
but she wasn't a brat.
She also loved to chitchat.

She loved hummingbirds,
and she was easy to be heard.
She also wasn't much of an early bird.

She loved coffee in her coffee pot,
especially when it was steaming hot.

She ought to have shot me,
'cause I'm a little snot.
Even though she taught me a lot.

Like it or not,
everyone should tell her...thanks a lot!

Trevan Price
Age: 11

DEAR GOD

Dear God, why did you take my brother from me?
In Heaven above where he's waiting for me
I can't wait to see
On a very pretty day in Clarksville
I can hear Momma say "Be careful Andrew!"
That's when you took my brother from me.

Dear God, my brother was perfect and nice
as you set our family on ice
the hate that builds inside our lives
as you stab us with your knives.

Dear God, how could you do this to me
me and my family
We're not giving you the blame
it's just a crying shame.

Dear God, on the way back from shopping
as the malls were hopping
The car got out of control
as the car flipped, and flipped, and flipped
as my heart flipped on its own.

Dear God, as I cry at his funeral
friends come to comfort me
Oh, why did you take him from me?

Dear God, as he's put in the ground
I remember the times, times that were happy
That made my life peppy.
Dear God, why did you take my brother from me?

Aimee Buntin
Age: 13

I WISH I HAD A FATHER

I wish I had a father
Someone who was there for me
Someone who would cheer me up
When I am feeling blue
Someone who would never leave me
Someone who cares for me
Someone that would love my two brothers, my mom,
And I forever and ever
I wish I had a father
A real father would be a perfect gift
But a father seems hard to find
It seems like no one is strong enough to take the
Responsibilities of one
Lots of boys pretend to be men
But it's just pretend
I can tell the difference
All they do is walk and walk out
I wish I had a father
But it'll never be

Rebecca K. Morr
Age: 11

THE FORGETFUL GIRL

Once there was a girl
Who could really twirl

But when she needed to know where something was
Her mind was just a fuzz

She asked her brother where are our fish
He had to tell her they were in a dish

She asked her dad where's the remote
He had to tell her it's in our boat

She asked her mom where is my brassiere
Her mom had to tell her I don't know my dear

Her family decided to call it quits
So the girl threw many fits

When at first she had to find things for herself
She had to look on every shelf

But after a while
She didn't have to walk a mile

She'd think where did I put that last
And she could find it very fast

R. Michael Brown
Age: 11

WHY DID IT HAPPEN TO YOU?

I woke that morning to find you were gone
How could it be
I said they were wrong
You were just so special to me

You were the sun in my sky
With your beautiful smile
All I can do is cry
I want to see you but it might be awhile.

The way you made me feel inside
The time was not right
But now you have died
Why did you have to die that night

While we are chasing dreams
You're in the dirt
And boy it seems
I can't hold back this hurt

I know you're up there
Shining down on me
I want you to know I care
But, boy, how could this be

Candice Hopkins
Age: 13

I WANT THAT DOLL!

Oh Cindy Marie, I know you want Suzy the doll
but we came for clothes at the mall

You have one just like her
at home in your winter fur

But this one has blue eyes
and mine has pink ties

Wouldn't you rather have pink ties
than ugly blue eyes

I want this one Mom!

Look it says she's made in Rome
and she looks so alone

Little Cindy Marie
you make me so angry

You will get it someday
between now and May

Now the time has come
and we must go home

For tomorrow is the big day
you will have dreams by a bay

Once you awake
there will be cake

For tomorrow is your birthday
and you will be served on a tray

NEXT DAY

Here is your birthday present
you better be pleasant

It's the doll
that I'd saw in the mall

(It's really her own doll
and not the one from the mall)

Oh thank you Mother
I want no other

Andrea Shackelford
Age: 12

AUTUMN

Hey the ground is brown.
The leaves are turning yellow, orange, brown.
Take that football over there.
Let's go on a hayride.
I'm bringing my jacket with me.
Hey do you want to build a bonfire.

Casandra LeAnn Sanford
Age: 9

MY FRIEND, MRS. R. B. HOOKS, SR.

As I walked slowly in the night,
I didn't feel quite right.
The first time I've been to a funeral home,
I sure would hate to be alone.

As I walked in the double door,
I felt like I couldn't take one step more.
I walked up to her son, Mr. Hooks.
He said, "At least she has better looks."

"And at least she's not in pain."
In that second strength I did gain.
My mom and I took a seat,
I tilted my head toward my feet.

I sat there and cried and cried
While I thought about the one who died.
When I was in kindergarten I read her a book,
When I finished, she gave me her happiest look.

We had the best relationship,
It was solid as a diamond and would never rip.
Then eight years later death came along.
I knew my predictions about
Our relationship were wrong.

Then I realized in my heart,
We still know each other, so we aren't that far apart.
I look forward to Heaven so I can see her again,
So we can let a better relationship begin.

Adam Kent Carson

BASEBALL

One day I played baseball and it was very fun
We ran and ran under the hot sun
Both teams were there with much delight
But still the sun was very bright
Players grabbed their bats and though they struck out
With a smile on their face went back to the dugout
As the pitcher got ready my mind went blank
With doubts in my mind I felt like I sank
The coach called my name quickly and fast
But by the time I looked up the ball had already past
A boy ran from third but he got out too
The reason for that is because he lost his shoe
The boy said to me "You should have
let the ball hit you!"
I said to him "At least I didn't lose my shoe!"
We went home with cokes in our hands
I took off my shoes and cut off the strands
I climbed into bed staring at the sun
When my mom came in and said
"At least you had fun!"

Ryan Wright
Age: 12

THE SHOW HEIFER

As I pass through the barn
on the morn of the big day.

As I gaze across the lots of the awaiting herd.
The moonlight glistens off the frosty pasture.

As we herd the heifers to their awaiting stalls
the clatter of their hooves sounds like
thunder from above.

As if they each know their own destination
they separate to their own private stalls.

As the daily routine begins by the placing of
the smooth nylon rope halter around the feminine
but stern neck of each beautiful heifer.

As we wait patiently our turn to enter the ring
the sunlight glistens off the red and black coats of
our prize-winning cattle.

The competition is steep but why should we fear
for our labor has been intense throughout the year.

As I present my heifer with her halter in my hand
the judge is marveled at how straight she stands.

As the judge marveled at the cattle that were
my competition with only one choice to make
that being my red heifer #1 second to none
the best the greatest Polled Charity.

Ethan Holloway
Age: 13

MRS. WHITE

Mrs. White,
Mrs. White.

She was so bright,
I always found the light.

She was funny,
But she always called me honey.

She was a good teacher for health,
One reason was she is healthy.

When I see her in the hall she hugs me,
But she does it carefree.

Still I'd like to thank her.

To: Mrs. White, the fourth grade teacher.

Adam Dale Johnson
Age: 11

LOVE GOES WITH PARENTS

Love goes with parents, as play goes with children.
Love is given away from our parents
no matter where they are.
Parents love you, even when you get in trouble.
They love you every minute.
They'll love you forever to bits.
You children should love them back.
Treasure your memories with them forever
and love them.

Laura Beth Galipeau
Age: 9

FOOTBALL

I like football,
I like when they tackle each other,
When they crash helmets it sounds like
they crack like coconuts.
I say, "Gosh, that had to hurt." Or I say, "Whoa!"
The buzzer honks like a horn on a truck.
I wish I could play,
but I would get smeared like a sandwich.
Or I'd get crushed like ice.

Brandon Nash
Age: 12

MR. B IS SPECIAL TO ME

Mr. B., Mr. B.,
He's the best that there can be.

Busy as can be.
Buzzing through the room.

Nothing gets by.
Mr. B's eye.
As quick as a flash.
He's on them.
Just like that!

Amanda Jane Lyons
Age: 12

SNOW

When I walk in the snow
it is like a white sandy beach
with footprints.
When it snows it is like a big white blanket
that covers the ground
When I go out onto the big white snow
it is heaven!

Laura Carter
Age: 12

RAINBOW

Sweeping gently through the sky,
Colorful streaks flying by,
Breaking through clouds,
Running through trees,
Who sees the rainbow?
Me!
Me!
Me!
Lucky charms,
A pot of gold,
When you're watching the rainbow,
You'll never grow old.
Some people say leprechauns paint
The candy-colored stripes flowing by.

Whitney Danielle Harper
Age: 11

COBRA

Poisonous
fast, cool, sleek, fascinating
The cobra is a very fast animal
long, scaly, colorful, keen
Cobra

Chase Nash

PAX

He is a sight to see,
Running wild and free.
Brown hair with a black tail and mane,
He nibbles ever so softly on his grain.
His mane hangs down between his eyes;
His tail swishes to get rid of the flies.
He has a playful look on his face
And always wants to quicken his pace.
When I ride, he runs like the wind.
Of all the things I know, he's my best friend.

Lindsey L. Harlan
Age: 13

Love is a romantic moment for two young people
who just got married.
They're both snuggled up together
by a fireplace kissing.
Love is a very sweet and special time.
Love is also caring about each other a lot.
Love is a time being together.

Amanda Lee Sharp
Age: 14

DEAR MOM

The only way I can put this
is that I'm never missed.

You're always there when I'm mad,
or when I'm just plain sad.

I'm just a pearl with a flaw,
but it only takes one call.

To find you and tell you that I miss you.
What can I say, but that I love you!

I don't know why I left you there,
with all the shedding of tears to bare.

You should be so proud of me once I'm better.
You will be happier than ever.

I'm on my way home now,
unless someone hits me with a pow.

Don't be afraid or scared for me
because right now, I've got only one plea.

I wish I could hurry up and come,
but for now, I'll start my letter with, "Dear Mom."

Brittney Huddleston
Age: 13

BASKETBALL

Basketball is fun
You have to be able to run, run, run

When you shoot a hoop and it goes in
Everyone says do it again

The object of the game
Is very simple, not insane

The object of the game
Is to dribble down the court
Shoot a three and win the game

But people think winning is all that
But having fun is better than that

And that is all
About basketball

So be cool
Stay in school
Play ball
And have fun

Matthew Morr
Age: 13

MICHAEL JORDAN

A special number is twenty-three.
A great basketball player is he.
With a first name Michael and Jordan as his last.

He's cool on the floor.
And man is he fast!!

Yes yes he's cool on the floor.
If you don't believe me just watch him soar!
He glides through the air.

With his Jordan shoes.
And all the crowd cheers.
As he dunkaroos.

Tyler Swift
Age: 8

SNOW

Snow is cold as ice
but still is very nice
Snow is a white blanket that covers
the ground
and it covers all around

Dusty Thomas

MY HEART IS BEATING VERY FAST

My heart is beating very fast,
At last!
A guy who likes me!

Oh my! My guy has let me down.
I really ought to tell you,
I shouldn't be in town.

I don't want cookies,
I don't want cake,
I definitely don't want a heartache!

My heart is beating very fast,
Oh, but it won't last!

Kaity Wheeler
Age: 8

Christmas is a time of giving and sharing
children peeking at their presents
parents shopping grabbing gifts as fast as they can
children running as fast as a car
trying to see what kind of goodies
they have gotten for Christmas.
Chestnuts roasting by the open fire
as stockings are so full they are busting.

Josh Wilson

STARS

My favorite star is the North Star
The North Star is very far

I cannot make things out of the stars
I have not even seen any cars

Have you seen the Big Dipper
I have not seen it but I've seen Flipper

I love the stars
And I like candy bars

I think there are some superstars
And they live on Mars

The superstars have some capes
And they can bake cakes

Some stars have names
Some play games

Some stars go to bed
Some have a sleepy head

Anne Macy Chambers
Age: 9

LIFE AFTER DEATH

Death can come at anytime
Demolishing, destroying
The soul, body, and mind
Amazingly and anxiously
Causing everyone to wonder why
Creeping up like a cat out of an alley
It can come silently or loudly
Coming from the front or the behind
It may kill your body
But it will leave your spirit to pry
So when you're feeling down and depressed
"About a death"
Just close your eyes
And you will soon come to realize
By truly loving and believing
Within your heart the soul shall never die
So when you're thinking of the person that's dead
Remember to always keep a high head
And don't forget this one last tip
To think of a death just like this

Dara D. Moorman
Age: 12

HOPE FOR LOVE

I would go outside and look up at the stars
   And I would see his face
smile at me while I'm smiling back
And in my head I would be thinking maybe
   we would be together someday
I also wonder when he comes out at night
   And look at the stars he would see
my face smiling at him while he's smiling at me
   but we should never give up hope
we'll be together someday

Laura Atherton
Age: 14

TEACHERS

Teachers are nice.
Teachers are clean.
They teach us stuff.
We tell them things.
They teach us our whole lives,
and then we have the privilege
to call them our friend.
Because they took the time
to teach us again and again.

Krista Cropper
Age: 12

O.M.S.

OMS is fun for all,
for people big and small.
So what if the food isn't all that good.
And our janitors are the best!
Especially Alton,
He never lets it rest.
The teachers are the bomb but,
they sometimes can act like our moms.
We the students are cool,
'cause we go to Owensboro Middle School!!!

Jessica Wooldridge
Age: 12

IF I WAS RICH

If I was rich I'd buy me a house,
I'd buy me some cats to keep out the rats
I'd buy me a horse and a dog
and when we ate we'd eat like slobs
I'd knock down the schools
and make no rules
I'd buy me the toy store
and I'd pray to the Lord
but one sure thing is
I'd never be bored.

Natalie Johnson
Age: 10

A FUNNY WAY OF FISHING

Once I went fishing without a fishing pole,
So I tied some string onto my big toe.

I jumped into the water and the fish jumped ashore,
So I hopped back out and I tried it once more.

The fish were so scared on that very day,
That they packed their bags and swam away.

I thought it might help to let you know,
To not take after me and fish with your toe!

Bradley A. Reynolds
Age: 13

WHEN THE WINDOWPANE CLATTERS

Does it matter when the windowpane clatters
the rain falling and streets filled with batter
does it really matter when the windowpane clatters
trucks roaming by but nothing's the matter
so don't have a fuss
just wait for the bus
just sit there listen to the clatters
but remember nothing's the matter.

Rachel Gabbert
Age: 9

MY ROSE LOVE TREE

I tried to say I love you
But it wouldn't come out of my mouth
It seems someone came to me
And stole it from my rose love tree
That says all my love things for me
But now I'm not afraid and
Now you hear me clear
I love you forever and always
And now I know I don't need a rose love tree
To say my love things for me

Allen Barger
Age: 12

TEACHERS HELP ME LEARN

Teachers help me learn.
They help me learn a lot.
When I have a little trouble,
they get me back in shape.

They help me learn my A,B,C's.
They also help me learn my 1,2,3's.
They help me learn my adding, subtracting,
division, and multiplication too.

Eric Scott Inscoe
Age: 11

FEELINGS

Awakening my passion
flowing over my face
bending my composure
quickening my pace

Forcing harsh words
reversing my smile
awakening new thoughts
cramping my style

Boggling my mind
juggling my emotions
twisting my body
controlling my notions

Reddening my face
determining my state
teasing my heart
dictating my fate

Tara Tomes
Age: 12

REMEMBER WHEN?

Morgan --

Remember when you were born?
  We spent the whole day and night,
at the hospital
  Being hazy and slumping down in our chairs
just waiting for you.
  Remember when you arrived,
you were white as a ghost?
  And the doctor had to hit you to make you
breathe?

Now you spend your days at home,
  Watching every move we make,
Trying to explore your home,
  And the voices of your family.
Now you're just a runt,
  But you will grow to be,
Just like me.

(For my little sis)

Amber N. Jones
Age: 11

THE OWL

The owl's wings
were burning in the
gray, angelic armor
of soft white feathers.

Soars through the heights
its battle cry,
a mere question

The owl asks
but never answers

Joey Gregory
Age: 12

SOMEONE

Who's the girl of my dreams
someone that's not perfect would be fine with me
someone that is kind and would care for me
someone that I could really get to know
someone that would be fine to show
someone that I could trust and depend on
someone that could be there to count on
someone that I can share my emotions with
someone...just someone that would be fine.

Blake Brasel
Age: 12

SPRINGTIME

For all my days I've been waiting,
waiting for spring to arrive.

I've been waiting for the beautiful gardens
full of flowers, and in that garden there will be
fantastic butterflies with all different colors.

For all my days I've waited for spring
to bring its wonderful sunshine to shine
and brighten my day, and to keep me warm.

Here I've been waiting,
waiting for so long for spring to come...
AND IT'S NOT HERE YET!!

Kim Harper
Age: 11

WHEW!

Old Farmer Johnny is no friend of mine
Even though he feeds me most all of the time
When fall is here
I disappear
Or be the main course when the kinfolks dine

Alisha Strange
Age: 10

WAITING FOR SPRING

Spring is when the groundhog awakes,
I hope he sees his shadow,
For if he doesn't it will be a late spring.

Spring is when the flowers start to bloom,
The weather gets warmer,
And the snow has all melted away.
Children play outside with friends,
Without getting a runny nose.

But here we are in the house,
Drinking hot chocolate,
With a runny nose,
Because it is just winter now.

Jerry Price
Age: 11

OH, CRY TO THOU NIGHT

Oh sigh by night,
And sing by day,
With no sight
There are no prayers for us to say.

If we cannot take,
We will bring to thou ocean,
It's not for us to take
With our full devotion.

With thou heart,
And not with thou soul,
Forever not to part,
From an unworthy old foe.

If you will not take thou,
We shall fight,
If you shall not know how
Oh cry to thou night.

Jay Stevenson
Age: 11

THE BIRD

There was a bird
Who didn't know how to fly
Then he saw his mother
Fly so very high

He tried to leap off the tree
But didn't go very far
He started to fall to the earth
Then hit a pretty car

The owner got very mad
And started to swear
He saw the scratch on his car
Then pulled out all his hair

Gregory A. Free
Age: 12

DREAMS

When you're awake
And you feel stressed
Or you feel worried
Go to sleep, dream a dream
You can go to a place you've never been
You can fly on a carpet you can sail on the sea
You can be other people you can be you or me
An igloo you might live in, or a teepee if you wish
Drink a chocolate milkshake or eat your favorite dish
But always remember, when you wake up
You might have those worries
Go back to sleep, dream another dream

Mason Kenneth Cornell

FEARS

I am running from
I know not what
It scared me then
I'm frightened
But as I run,
I see what scared me.
What turned out
To be my fear
Was being afraid
Of being afraid

Charles R. DeVillier
Age: 11

JESUS WITHIN

He hung on the cross with nails in hands,
To give his life for us to live on the lands,
He loved us dearly,
And the whole world loves him almost nearly,

If thou loveth him, thou shall not perish,
For he loves us and we shall forever cherish,
Adam and Eve were here long ago,
They are in Heaven and not down below,

I got this from the Bible,
I also like to be at revival,
Because I have Jesus within,
He washes away all of my sin.

Brandon Gish
Age: 11

FALL

Come on everybody let's all cheer,
Summer is gone and fall is here.
It's gonna be fun for you and me,
So many fall things to do and see.

Red and orange and yellow and brown,
These colors are seen all over town.
The leaves are pretty but not all fun,
Before the day ends, raking is done.

Jump in, jump in we will all say,
We're all gonna have fun today.
Jumping and playing in all of the piles,
Will surely give us all big smiles.

Shannon Fulkerson
Age: 9

THE BEST THING I LIKE ABOUT FALL

The best thing I like about fall
Is the changing of leaves from green to red.
They blow around
And land on your head.
The more you rake
The more that falls.
Keep on working until
Your mother calls.
This is the story of
Fall.

Andrew S. Deese
Age: 9

FALL

I was walking down the street,
as slowly as can be.
Until I saw this red leaf fall,
from a big maple tree.
I got excited,
because I knew it was fall.
I ran home fast,
to tell my mom.
Mom! Mom!
Fall is near.
All the fun holidays,
will soon be here.

Ashley N. Horn
Age: 10

WHY DID YOU MAKE ME
GET OUT OF BED MOM

Why did you make me get out of bed
Mom
Why did you make me get out of bed
Mom
Why make me go out into the world
Mom
Why not let me stay in bed
Mom
Why make me leave this peaceful
room
Why not let me be
Mom
Why did you make me get out of bed
Mom
Why can't I just stay and sleep

Christa Wear
Age: 12

BUBBY--

Remember when we played in the mud?
  We spent hours laughing in the golden sun!
Remember when we wrestled on the floor?
  You always thought you were the tough one!
Remember when we played with my dolls?
  I always thought you liked to do that!

Now you live over 1,000 miles away.
  I never see you anymore.
I always remember the times we spent laughing
  And
Crying together.
  Sometimes I cry and sometimes I laugh.
Won't you ever come home and do some of the
  Things we
Did before you left and went so far away?

                                    Jessica Wayne Lively
                                    Age: 11

I'M A LITTLE BUTTERFLY

I'm a little butterfly
eating a peach
I'm a little butterfly
lying on the beach
I'm a little butterfly
eating grapes
I'm a little butterfly
turning into shapes
I'm a little butterfly
falling to the ground
I'm a little butterfly
going as fast as sound
I'm a little butterfly
getting cold
I'm a little butterfly
dying in the snow.

Kristina C. Robertson
Age: 9

THANKSGIVING DAY

Thanksgiving day is one of the best times of the year.
When you really think about it, it's almost here.
Nobody really cares for the weather
On Thanksgiving day.
Thanksgiving is almost here.
Yay Yay Yay.

Kayla King

THE MOUNTAIN POOL

The day is cool,
By the mountain pool.
Up so high,
It touches the sky.
Down the mountain does it flow,
To the far off valleys down below.
When it reaches the bottom it is pure and clear,
And down deep in its water do children peer.
The children look for a treasure,
But what they find is truly pleasure!

Amanda Kirtley
Age: 9

THE LAST GOOD-BYE

With all our love
We'll fly like doves
Which we'll fly above
Where there will never be a single shove
We all have hearts sometimes they fall apart
When it's time we feel worthless like a dime
We'll turn into something that will shine
They were so really kind
Even though we might feel left behind.

To Grandma Smith. In memory of Grandpa Smith.
                    Sincerely,
                    Jeff

                              Jeff Smith
                              Age: 10

WHEN I SAW A WITCH

Hello little kiddy
How do you do
If you didn't know
I'm going to put a spell on you
I'll put you in my stew
With my other kiddies too
I started to run to my house
Then I saw an enormous mouse
I started to scream,
But then I awoke from my dream.

Allie Edge
Age: 10

EVERYBODY KNOWS THE CLAUS

Don't you smell the cookies bakin',
Can't you see that belly it's a shakin',
Don't take a cookie off the pan,
You don't want to mess with this man,

You've never seen this side of him before,
You know he won't be knockin' at your door,

Here comes Santa Claus,
Doin' all those good things,
Cruisin' down the air highway in his sleigh,
Bringing all the presents for the next day,

His cookies and his milk are his pride,
Or anything that can be deep-fried,
Don't get me wrong he's a real nice guy,
But you don't want to get on his bad side.

Victoria Beadnell
Age: 12

HORSE

Horse
huge, muscular
galloping, hurdling, leaping
go to the Kentucky Derby
Will Snowball win?

Kathryn Nicole Daugherty

THE TURKEY BLUES

Taylor Turkey was so cute
He got married and lost his loot
Taylor married a chick
Out he was kicked
Now Taylor plays the blues on his flute

Angel Strobel

German shepherd
intelligent, powerful
hunts, runs, growls
it lives in Britain
so far away

Zachery Heath Baughn
Age: 9

MR. TURKEY

Hello, I'm Mr. Turkey I'm happy as can be
'Til Thanksgiving day I'll be safe you'll see
You will hear me from town to town
There will be heads rolling around
I'm sorry to say it will be me.

Audrey Higdon

Pilgrims
brave, religious
sailed, suffered, built
worked hard to live
Pioneer

Heather Norwood
Age: 9

CLARK PERKY TURKEY

Clark the perky turkey
Lived in Albuquerque
He had a good past
Except Thanksgiving last
Now he's not as perky

Maggie McKay

EVENING

Sun low in the sky
white fluffy cotton ball clouds
float above my head
bright red roses
catch my eyes
sweet fragrance of honeysuckle
from the field across the road
butterflies putter
birds sing "tweet tweet"
oh, what a sweet sound
big, black, lumpy clouds
sneak over my head
the sun disappears

It is night.

Jessica Gael Roby
Age: 9

I AM A BASKETBALL PLAYER

I am a basketball player.
I shoot free throws.
I practice every day.
I dribble at home.
I am a basketball player.

I run to the other end.
I sweat every game.
I yell to my teammate to throw me the ball.
I pass to other teammates of mine.
I am a basketball player.

I play aggressive.
I guard the other team.
I rebound the ball.
I throw the ball to the net.
I am a basketball player.

I hear the cheers.
I listen to the buzzer.
I always look at the scoreboard.
I hear the whistle.
I am a basketball player.

Samantha Eversole
Age: 10

I AM A WATER SPORTSMAN

I am a water sportsman.
I put my skis on.
I hold my breath as the boat pulls me out of the water.
I glide across the water.
I fall when I get tired.
I am a water sportsman.

I rev up the motor of the jet ski.
I jump the waves.
I bust my tooth.
I feel severe pain.
But, I am still a water sportsman.

I crawl on the tube.
I jump the wake.
I flip when I hit the water.
I float until the boat comes back.
I swim to the tube again.
I am a water sportsman.

T. Benjamin Vincent
Age: 9

I AM A PUPPY LOVER!!!

I am a puppy lover.
I like to play with him.
I walk my puppy every day.
I support my puppy.
I am a puppy lover.

I enjoy my puppy.
I take good care of him.
I bathe him when he gets real dirty.
I give my puppy good things.
I am a puppy lover.

I like my puppy because he's the best.
I am going to keep him forever.
I walk my puppy up and down the yard.
I am a puppy lover.

I love my puppy very much.
I let my dad ride him in the back of the truck
    because I can't.
I will always love my puppy.
I am a puppy lover.

Lee Ann Keith
Age: 10

There was a boy
That thought he was a toy
He was a fool
He thought he was cool
His last name was Coy.

Ashley Danielle Simpson

DARKNESS

Darkness
is so very dark
the stars come out to show
the stars come out to give you light
Darkness!

Melissa Clark

LIFE

Sometimes the days are rough,
But that just makes us tough
There are lessons to be learned,
And lessons to be taught
Life doesn't last forever
So you know what you should do,
Take the opportunities in life
And use them wisely
So life will be worth waking up to.

Lacey Geary

TOM TURKEY

Big, fat and covered with feathers and called Tom
In November I'm runnin' from everyone's mom
I ended up in the oven
Now, I'm a meal everyone's lovin'
A Thanksgiving without me is sure to be a bomb.

Kendal Wethington
Age: 10

I AM A CHRISTIAN

I am a Christian
I read the Bible
I listen to my preacher.
I watch my Bible tape.
I obey God.
I am a Christian.

I love church.
I pray to God.
I come to church.
I don't stop loving Jesus.
I am a Christian.

I come to God.
I get happy when I hear about Jesus.
I would love to see him.
I love Jesus' birthday.
I am a Christian.

Molly Stewart
Age: 9

AIR

Air is polluted
from some stacks come big smoke clouds
help save our clean air

Thomas W. Patrick

I AM A BOOKWORM

I am a bookworm.
I hope I get more books.
I read every book I can.
I go home and read a book every day.
I am a bookworm.

I get my hands on any book I can.
I grab every book I can.
I dash to the book isle when I go to the store.
I take good care of my books.
I am a bookworm.

I hate when I can't read a book.
I like it when I get a book.
I love to read.
I don't like my books being taken away.
I am a bookworm.

Charles Lance Piper
Age: 9

Indians
wise, creative
hunting, dancing, singing
a very spiritual group
Native Americans

LaPorsha Richards
Age: 10

I AM A GO-CARTING KID

I am a go-carting kid.
I crank up the motor.
I hate it if the motor doesn't start.
I heat up the motor.
I am a go-carting kid.

I speed up hills.
I don't go fast enough and I spin out.
I zoom through the woods.
I crash into a stump.
I am a go-carting kid.

I push harder on the gas.
I yell when I go down a hill.
I scream when I crash.
I turn too sharp and flip it.
I am a go-carting kid.

Justin Dwayne Lambert
Age: 9

THE DAY I HAD TO SIT

I'm Little Ricky,
my name is on the board.
I hit little Johnny Boy,
tripped over a cord.
I have to miss break.
Mrs. Coomes ate my cheesecake.
I had no one to play with
or nothing to do.
Why did I have to hit little Johnny Boy?

James Dale Wills
Age: 10

Wolves
cunning, furious
hunting, howling, sleeping
watching the pack
keeping the pack secure

Joshua Robert Hall
Age: 10

Fall
chilly, breezy
sparkling, glowing, crunching
red, yellow, orange leaves
beautiful season
Autumn

April Basham
Age: 9

THANKSGIVING DAY

On Thanksgiving day my family has fun,
Watching children eat, play, and run.
Sometimes we play football in the sun,
But when it gets dark, the fun is done!

Brittany Stephens

FALL

My favorite season of them all,
Is the one and only fall.
Yellow, red and orange I spy,
When they die in a pile I'll lie.
In the fall I smell hot apple pie.
And I smell caramel apple too.
You will see the nice blue sky,
You will hear the word "boo!"

Dean Stitz
Age: 10

THE CORNER

Mom sat me here for punishment,
I can't get up at all,
Until I'm very sorry for marking on her wall,
And if I sit here forever 'cause I'm so sad today,
Don't laugh at me while I'm in this chair,
And don't wipe my tears away.

Joshua T. Wendt
Age: 9

THE GAME

Running, dribbling down the court
Hoping that my shot's not short,
Time's running out, we've got to score,
I pass the ball to number four.
His shot falls short, I'm on the board
I tip it in, hooray we win!

Craig Bchnkc
Age: 10

Kitten
small, big
springing, rolling, running
They get stuck in a bowl.
How will they escape?

Heather Schroader
Age: 9

SUMMER FUN

Summer is fun
so bright in the sun.
School is out
I feel like a shout.
I am going out to play.
I really love this day.
Now it is night
the stars are so bright.

Misty Johnson
Age: 9

DREAMING

Ms. Jones asks me, "What's 9 x 3?"
Oops! Oh no! I was dreaming.
"Huh?" I ask her sheepishly.
Her face turns red and she yells at me.

I look at the ground, listening.
I look up. She's glaring at me.
She goes back to her teaching.
I go back to my dreaming.

Whitney Wilgus
Age: 11

You're a sick old pup.
Nobody could get you up.
You just sit around all day.
In your sick old way.
You're a sick old pup.

Aaron Cockrill
Age: 12

Panda bear
chubby, black-circled eyes
live in China, look like raccoons, get frightened
trapped in a gigantic net.
How will they escape?

Danielle Kramer
Age: 10

THE SOCK!

I saw a shadow creeping in my house,
It was quiet and had the sound of a mouse.
I stood and yelled who's there,
Then my brother grabbed me unaware.
I was scared, and frightened with a bit of shock,
My brother said I just wanted to give you this sock.

Vickie Hale
Age: 13

SCOUTING

I am a Cub Scout and
I'll tell you what it is all about
On Mondays the scouts meet as a den
And next week we meet again
When I go to camp I take along my night lamp
When I cook over an open fire
A burnt hot dog is something to admire
If you want to camp outside
Be a Cub Scout and do it with pride

Jacob Hicks
Age: 9

THE DEAD TURKEY

Max was playing with Jay
When the farmer came out to say
You had better hide ol' turkey
Or you'll be beef jerky
But Max and Jay were prey that day

Jackie Lanham
Age: 10

WHAT THAT COW SAID

Cows are yummy,
cows are sweet,
cows are meat that you can eat,
cows are smooth
cows are cool they don't go to school.
You kick-em in the ribs and they go moo.
Cows are fantastic they aren't spastic.

David Hunt
Age: 14

THE OLD TURKEY

There was on old turkey in the yard,
Who was playing with real cards.
The farmer was all out of breath,
Because the turkey scared him to death.
That was a day that was really hard.

Jonathon Brown
Age: 10

STARS

You go outside and there they are,
Up in the sky and way afar
The stars say we call them shiny
So bright you can see them at sunset and late
at night.
Sometimes we can't see them but they are
always there;
They look as though they would float
everywhere.
We wake up in the morning and they have
disappeared,
But don't worry they'll be back every day of
the year.

Kevin Earl Mathews
Age: 12

TIMMY THE TURKEY

Timothy Turkey was once a stray
Who tried to look fatter than a turkey may
His stomach somehow popped
And his heart soon stopped
So he flopped down and lain on that sunny day

Hannah Lewis
Age: 11

LOUISE

The birds, the bees
I'll fall to my knees
I love you O' Sweet Louise

I'll drive you around
Take you to town
Unless you make me frown

If I ever become a man
I'll love you as much as I can
Hey, do you have a tan

Virgil Singleton
Age: 13

MY FINGERNAILS

My nail polish is a part of me
The colors I have are purple,
yellow, blue and iguana green
glitter, pink, red, and meteorite
sounds like something that glows at night.

I don't like fake nails
they are uncomfortable
but I have a friend who actually
wears them at school.

I have a nail dryer but
the batteries went dead
so I'll have to air dry
my wet nails instead.

I guess it is crazy looking stuff
but I think it's cool and that's enough.

Felicia Leeann Gay
Age: 11

DEAD TURKEY

There was an old turkey named Bill.
He tried to run up the hill.
But he had a stroke.
His old heart broke.
So they ended up reading his will.

Ben Hayden
Age: 10

FALL

Summer has passed,
And now it's fall.
Baseball was a blast.
Now it's time for football.
Right around the corner is Halloween.
I might be a devil, but not a queen.
I'll dress in red and black,
And have a tail upon my back.

Jeffery David Hart
Age: 9

NAMES

Chris, Chris, That's my name
Chris, Chris, I like to play games
Chris, Chris, I eat grain
Chris, Chris, I like my bread plain
Chris, Chris, I like my name.

Becky, Becky, That's my mom's name
Becky, Becky, She likes her bread plain
Becky, Becky, She has a cat
Becky, Becky, She has a hat
Becky, Becky, She likes her name.

Bob, Bob, That's my dad's name
Bob, Bob, He likes his bread plain
Bob, Bob, He doesn't like to play games
Bob, Bob, He likes to eat beans
Bob, Bob, He likes his name.

Chris Bowersock
Age: 11

WILD FLOWER

W is for the wide variety in which they come.
I is for their intense colors for which they belong.
L is for the lovely fragrance that they give the world.
D is for the daring places they fruitfully grow.

F is for the floriferous quality that they possess.
L is for the many shaped leaves
   that hang onto the stems.
O is for the obvious beauty that they have.
W is for the wonderful numbers of them.
E is for the exciting heights that they reach.
R is for the rarity of times that they are appreciated.

Wild flowers frequent the earth, but often are not seen.

Kory Helmick
Age: 10

FALL

Fall, fall is something nice and cool,
my little baby niece likes to drool.
All the candy,
is quite dandy.
My sister can be scary,
and my brother can be very hairy.

Jessica Riggs
Age: 10

My dog is tan and yellow,
And he's really a handsome fellow
I taught him how to do tricks,
But he'd much rather chew on sticks
Spot barks all night long,
Even until the clocks says "DINGDONG"
My dog is loud, but sweet,
And I love the way he licks my feet
Without my dog I would cry,
Especially if I didn't get to say,
"GOOD-BYE."

Stephanie N. Brown
Age: 12

FALL

Fall is here,
Cool weather is near.
The leaves are turning brown,
They're falling to the ground.
Thanksgiving is coming,
We'll go turkey hunting.
For fall is here,
My favorite time of the year.

Christopher Armstrong
Age: 10

F ather is a person who cares for you in
    good times and bad.
A father is a person that loves you at all times.
T he best father is a good father.
H elping you with homework is one of the many things
    they do for you.
E very kid needs a father.
R espect your father no matter who it is.

Chris Thompson
Age: 10

TEACHING CHILDREN TO THINK AND DREAM!

Some teachers are nice.
Some teachers are mean.
We give them hopes.
They give us dreams.

They teach us things,
That we need to know;
To help us live and to grow.

So if you see one sometime,
Thank them greatly for the
Knowledge and rhymes.

Thank a teacher.
Hug a teacher.
Or even give them a wink.
Show them your appreciation.
For teaching children to think.

Angie Kennedy
Age: 11

THE MAN IN RED

The snow is falling upon the trees,
Please, dear Santa, don't forget about me!
My tree is up, with lights so bright,
Just waiting for you on Christmas night.

Can't wait to hear those sleigh bells ring,
With your reindeer ripping through the wind.
Loaded with toys for every girl and boy,
We wish you peace, happiness and joy.

Santa, I can hear your ho, ho, ho's,
As you slide down the chimney hole.
Your cookies and milk are on the table,
There's hay for the reindeer in the stable.

Jason Blanton
Age: 9

ARE THERE SUCH THINGS AS WINNERS?

Everyone loves to win and be recognized.
Some are more competitive than others,
But nobody likes to lose.
Often it seems you can't win for losing.

Winners are usually in the limelight
And have high expectations.
Watched extremely close, every mistake magnified.
Life can become stressful when
Winning is the only outcome.

Winners always have someone trying to top them.
Someone pushing them to work even harder.
If a winner slips up and loses, their talents are doubted.

Winners always have someone jealous of them.
Someone who creates rumors
And disrupts their thoughts.
Therefore a winner is sometimes on his own.

Winners have followers pretending
To be in their corner.
When they achieve success, their so called "friends"
Are always there to share in the glory.

If they come up short, their "friends"
Are nowhere to be found.

Winners will undoubtedly be losers at times.
What isn't understood, is that winners
Aren't afraid to fail.
They look forward to the challenge of a new day.

Are you a winner?

Benjamin Paul Rushing
Age: 15

HALLOWEEN! HALLOWEEN!

Halloween! Halloween!
Such a frightening scene.
Ghost! Ghost!
Such a scary host.
Witches! Witches!
Licking their stitches.
Parties! Parties!
People not using their smarties.

Brandon Kyle Roberson
Age: 10

HALLOWEEN TRICKSTERS

Three Halloween tricksters are we;
My brother, my sister, and me.
We walk down the streets,
Playing tricks and getting treats.

Jennifer Haut
Age: 9

TIGER

Orange, black, beautiful
Hunts prey during jungle nights
For its survival

Justin Sparkman
Age: 13

AUTUMN CHANGES

I crunch the leaves beneath my feet;
the smell of fall is so so sweet.
Leaves are sprawled all over the ground.
The wind is blowing them wildly around.
The trees are so very bare;
it's kind of hard not to sit and stare.

Amanda Sherfey
Age: 11

MOMS

Moms are as sweet as a sucker
Moms are as warm as a blanket
and as cuddly as a stuffed fluffed bear
and they clean up after us on and off
on and off.
Moms are so beautiful that they catch my sight
they are so beautiful.
Moms know it all and they smell as good as roses!!!

Brittney Rippy
Age: 11

TIME

The hands on a clock,
move by each number
Ticking, silently, and slowly.
Although you know time flies by,
the hands on a clock,
move around slowly.
Letting the good times last forever.

Kim Kneepkens
Age: 12

WINTER

Winter is snowmen standing in the snow
Winter is when little sparkles fall on my nose
Winter is when tiny stars fall from the sky
Winter is when you should sing this lovely lullaby

Rachel Morris
Age: 9